Channing's Note-Book

Passages from the Unpublished Manuscripts of William Ellery Channing

Selected by his Granddaughter

Grace Ellery Channing

Boston
American Unitarian Association
1902

IN adding this little volume to the published works of William Ellery Channing, a special interest is claimed for it from its origin and character.

The "Notes" are from the unpublished manuscripts left by him, and set apart for this purpose by his nephew and biographer, William Henry Channing, and by his son. They have been gathered with careful study, and are here reproduced, without change or revision of any kind. Many of them bear internal evidence of this in their abrupt construction. So far has the desire to preserve their integrity been carried that it is only justice to the publishers to exonerate them from all responsibility for incomplete sentences or idiomatic use of words.

What is possibly lost in elegance is more than compensated in vigor and freedom of expression. Written for personal and immediate reference, the papers have the absolute unrestraint of self-communion; yet we feel that in giving them to the world no injustice is done to the writer. He loses nothing through this nearer acquaintance.

It was Dr. Channing's habit to make notes at all times, to jot down the train of thought suggested by the books he was reading, as well as his own solitary musings. Often words or phrases from other writers are set down with the ideas they suggest; and sometimes it has been difficult to disentangle the two. The most faithful care has been employed to reject such passages. Should any have escaped, the fault must be attributed to the compiler.

Many thoughts will be recognized as familiar; the form, however, is believed to be new, and we think, as a book distinctly *not* theological in character, it presents another and broader view of Channing himself.

The selections which close the volume, beginning with "Sensation," are from the chapters of his unfinished work on Man, which was designed to be the crowning labor of his life. Nearly half a century has elapsed since these pages were penned, and it will not be strange if no great or striking novelty is found, at the present day, in the philosophy they embody; but they show most fully the spiritual thought which was so far in advance of his own time, and emphasize anew the special characteristics of Channing's mind and faith. Therefore, as well as for their beauty, they are included in this volume.

To those here and across the water whose lives are bound up with all movements for freedom, this little book, as a voice for individual liberty, will carry its own special welcome; and to the friends of Channing everywhere it is offered.

GRACE ELLERY CHANNING.

CONTENTS.

———◆———

DR. CHANNING'S NOTE-BOOK.

Freedom.

FREEDOM is not merely a means. It is an end. It is the well-being of a rational nature. To take it away is to violate the essential law and aspiration of that nature.

If there be one interest dear to me on earth, it is the freedom of the human mind. If I have found my existence a growing good, — if I have gained any large views of religion or my own nature, — if I have in any measure invigorated, I know nothing to which, under God, I am so indebted as to my freedom. This has been breath of life to me.

The abuses of freedom are better than chains, for they are self-corrective. Man should always feel himself too great to be a slave.

Forego everything, rather than invest another with the power of determining your actions, or transfer to him the empire which belongs only to our own minds.

Each man being a law to himself, he cannot be a slave to others.

Worlds should not tempt me to bend my mind to the yoke which Christians here bear. I owe too much to intellectual liberty. If I have made any progress, — here the spring.

Civil liberty is not enough. There may be a tyranny of the multitude, of opinion, over the individual. He is free who is most encouraged to consult his highest nature and to act from it. Popularity enslaves. We want no limits to the range of the human mind.

How many have fought for civil liberty with not a glimpse of true freedom!

I let the bird go whose songs I desire, because the life and joy of liberty are his element and true good.

In so doing I set free every slave, — I wish for each being his true element and good.

The necessities of nature leave us no liberty. How we act on traditional rules, maxims, customs! How few think for themselves! How many depend for light!

Liberty is not an animal license.

Man.

I am never to lose the consciousness of my own importance as an intellectual and moral being. Whoever respects it is my friend. I deserve this respect.

Neglect, contempt, indifference, are all improper towards such a being as Man.

How far are men kept in wickedness by being taught that it is their natural state !

Must not all ambition die when we see the Divine likeness in all souls ? Before this, slavery and war fall.

The misery of mankind is not this or that calamity, but ignorance of the true resources from all calamity.

In injuring a man the injury is not measured by the pain inflicted, but by the *being* injured.

Man, if he make virtue his chief end, can turn all things into *means*.

The gift of reason and consciousness make a being who is to govern himself : — he is only to be restrained when he would injure others.   He has a great destiny which he only can fulfil.

Every human being has a right to all the means of improvement which society can afford.

Obstinacy comes sometimes from a *half*-view of human dignity, and then it is better than pliancy.

Do we not feel a man to be great just in proportion as he forms himself, — retreats into himself for guidance and adheres to what his own soul pronounces to be right and good ?

Man is at once a social and a religious being. Religion cannot flourish without charity, nor the reverse.   Man is a mutilated being when destitute of either sentiment.

He who searches himself with the distinct conviction that he is a being framed and gifted for universal love will join the deepest humility to the most unbounded aspirings.

Every man cannot do everything for himself. He must be helped.   But the end of being helped is that he may act more energetically.   The man who is always receiving aids, instead of conferring them, is a poor creature.

A man was not made merely to enjoy, — the higher end is character. A condition making him merry, but degrading him, is the worst. It is well that degradation should bring misery.

Every soul is great — unspeakably so.

Man's nature is now divided. Body wars against soul. A new reverence for the body is needed, — such as will protect it from foreign violence.

Show masks a nature meant for greatness.

There is no feeling of obligation to accomplish the purposes of human nature.

Man cannot control outward nature, — he can do more, he can rise above it. In all changes he can hold his steadfast course. He can adhere to the great and good, though opposed by the universe.

The lowest, most ignorant, man is to be treated with respect. Not because we are worthless, but because we are so noble. Our own development of powers should only awaken a livelier concern towards those in whom the Divine ray slumbers.

Man everywhere fights against man. The attempt to eclipse another is an act of hostility. — Love has infinite obstacles.

To give a generous hope to man of his own nature, is to enrich him immeasurably.

I am not to ask or expect God to determine my mind.   That is my proper work.

Learn to view earthly distinctions as trifling. See in every rank, MAN.

The great man among the great will show less than a far inferior man among the little.

Men are sinful just as they are foolish, and good just as they are wise, — i. e., very mixed in both respects.

Avoid undue severity.   Call a man a harder name than he merits, and you so far confirm him in error and create sympathy *with* him.

What have you lost?   Everything essentially precious is left you, for your own nature is left you.   Had a calamity fallen on you which had robbed you of the attributes of reason, or annihilated the principle of duty, or the Idea of God, or the capacity of pure love, — then you would have incurred an infinite loss.   Over such a calamity, no weeping would be excessive, but the misfortunes of the day — what have they taken?

Associate man with God. Plead for him as he has never been pleaded for before.

Society — the State.

I owe so much to my country that I cannot, ought not, to be indifferent to its interests.

Republicanism does not know itself. It is highest spiritualism. It is the rejection of all outward distinction. It honors man as man.

The people have a right to be well governed. They have a right to judge whether they are, — and, if convinced they are not, they have a right to change the government.

A bad sovereign makes an unhappy country. Does this rule change when the people are sovereign? Can the people govern any farther than they are enlightened and self governed? The people swayed by demagogues do *not* rule.

Despotism is a cure for parties. Shut up men's mouths and minds, and all will agree, but who wishes thus to banish party spirit? In free governments we shall have variety of thoughts, views. The free mind is still a blessing.

It is the distinction of a statesman from a

politician that he sees, comprehends and seizes on the enduring, the stable, the eternal, — that low temporary interests do not hide the everlasting.

Nothing but sympathy with society will lead to its cure. Hence those who are raised above the mass can do little.

No man has a claim to office but on grounds of spiritual distinction.

Man's right to his productive power is higher, more universal than all others.

Every individual has a right to vote, as each has an interest in government and is an end of government. This interest is expressed by his individual action in the government.

How we fold up ourselves in our comforts and respectablenesses! How little we dream what surrounds us!

The suppression of the multitude by *force* is not *order*. It is *rebellion kept down.*

We lead self-contradictory lives, — admit ideas of justice, but do not apply them, declaim against degrading labors, but avail ourselves of them.

Wealth worship *must* cease.

Employments degrading to others are crimes. No man has a right to grow rich, employing people in ways which brutalize them.

Why should not property be taken care of by government, rather than other things? Why ~~not~~ science, arts, virtue?

What does it indicate that we pass suffering in the streets without noticing it, — see human misery, destitution, degradation, and not heed it?

Society is a war of force for the protection of individuals. What has this war achieved, what murder, oppression!
Is it safe to accumulate physical force in any hands?

It is of no importance that there should be a rich man in the community, but of great importance that there should not be a poor one. Affluence does good to none. Pauperism does evil to all.

To elevate employments, remove debasing circumstances, is a great duty. Let every being have means and aids to improvement.
That others may be better for serving us should be our end.

How near must a person live to me to be my neighbor? Every person is near to you whom you can bless. He is nearest whom you can bless most.

Men are toiling perpetually for ease. They ask for a social order which will give them security. They try to fence off the evils of life by their gains, their social connections, their social ranks. Let time flow easily. Let unpleasant questions be turned aside. Let nothing disturb them. This paradise of comfort and ease they sigh for. — But such is not the purpose of God.

When we look at the *influential*, the *respectable*, have we any ground of hope!

The present state of society is the creature of low, earthy minds. All sympathy with it then is perilous. The factitious, conventional, fashionable tone is essentially low. The whole era is tainted.

Life, when a drudgery for subsistence, seems to fall below the existence of animals; who sport, — take free range.

The people must not serve as pedestal for a great man.

What right have we to anything for ourselves, which would do greater good to others?

The whole tendency of the present state of things is to self-indulgence, — and this is a deadly atmosphere. He who would do good must not live in it.

Strange, with such a founder, example, as Washington, we so want faith in *moral* government.

Only a few of the laboring class can rise, for it is *by them* that any one rises.

All true society is the acting of one spirit on another, the communication of the activity of one soul to another.

The man living to amuse himself, who contributes nothing to the general movement, should be counted false to his trust, — to his race.

All vice is forging chains for a country. You, men of pleasure, are bowing us to a master.

In the present state of society must not the noblest be despised?

Is it right to make a display of wealth by which the poor are humbled in their own eyes, and by which their ideas of the happiness of higher conditions are perverted?

Nothing is so injurious as for a man to form himself on a state of society which he is called to *re*form.

How much of social intercourse consists of efforts to maintain one another's self complacency!

Our social nature should keep pace with the intellectual. To lose the power of communication by our solitary studies is very injurious.

The use of credit is that a man to get it must fulfil his contracts. It is a stimulus to fidelity.

I am no leveller. I have no favors to gather of the poor. I would accept no office they can give me. I ask no votes. I hold the doctrine of equality only on the ground of the capacity of souls. I have learned it not from demagogues, but from divine sages: a man who labors is fit for any society.

Of what avail good laws if men of property alone can use them, — if justice is too dear for the poor!

The idea of a whole, and general good, leads to what has done infinite mischief, — to the merging of the individual in a mass. This is infinitely corrupt.

SOCIETY — THE STATE. 19

To extinguish the moral life in a fellow creature is the greatest sin, — far greater than murder.

The unhappy man, reduced to dependence on alms, finds his lot a burden, and temptation too hard for common virtue, — whilst he who is threatened with indigence is powerfully drawn to seek refuge in crime.

It is murder to kill a man, but not to let him starve, and if, when starving, he steals, he may be justly punished !

Is not law sustained by personal reverence ? It is as well that the few, as the many, should rule, if both have the spirit of ruling.

Past powers are seized on by selfishness and sensuality. The energies spent for wealth would ennoble individuals and society.

We were made for something nobler than to get money. We do infinite dishonor to our minds and life to suppose that we have no higher work than to amass dust.

A high end in the community is an impulse which individuals can hardly withstand. Whatever the community *demands* will be done.

Were men in a brotherly spirit to join their forces for one another's defence, the forces of outward nature would harm them little. Universal justice and love would change the earth, with all its storms and droughts, into paradise.

Man's selfishness is more withering than drought, his passions more desolating than floods, his excesses more deadly than disease.

Our business is not to find fault with the world discontentedly. It is the world in which God has placed us, — therefore the best for us, and we should apply ourselves to the work of reforming it cheerfully, joyfully.

Ideas, passively received from abroad, do little good. Is not this the hardship of the multitude — that the spring within is not touched?

We cannot eradicate humanity. We are never to think the link severed which binds us to all. To feel its power when weakened, — to be drawn to others in whom humanity is obscured, — this is glorious!

We keep one another down, when our only aim should be to lift up one another.

Sentiment does more than force.

In our attempts to conciliate the world we lose all our energy.

He is the pleasing companion who gives activity to other minds.

In respecting one right we are learning to respect all.

Hard work is for many a sterner despot than an absolute king.

Wealth is power over others. Ought not this, like all power, to be limited?

We melt whole multitudes into one mass, — call them a country, — England, — etc., and hate and fight them. Ought we not to dissolve all these, to see people as human beings?

This association into nations, — is it to endure forever?

You owe your leisure to the man who works. Then study for him. You are his debtor. You owe your mind to him — then use your mind for him — give it. This is the great duty.

No man, I hold it, has a right to improve himself for himself only. He improves through the laborers who have transmitted ancient knowledge. We need different classes — but each for all!

We should help others to discover truth. To hide power through love, to teach without humbling, — this is beautiful. How little the right of our brothers is respected! How much oppressing of the spirit to which we ought to give freedom!

It is a sign of infancy when only a few beings interest us.

The more undoubted a person's rank is, the more easily he can condescend; for no one can form the idea of his being on a level with inferiors whom he notices. Hence there is little real condescension!

Is any class of men to be so honored as those who espouse the cause of the most friendless, and who can gain nothing but reproach, — who make no compromise with opinion?

I have seen men whose whole souls seemed smothered by the idea of property. When they saw another man, the first idea seemed to be, how much is he worth?
All the magnificence of a nature shrinks before property.

It is sometimes easier to give than to be just. Giving implies superiority. Equity acknowledges another's claims as rights.

Slavery.

A man comprehends a *human being*. I would no more think of owning him than of owning earth or Heaven.

We must strike at the root of slavery, — unconsciousness of the dignity of the human being.

Slavery is a branch of the general contempt of human nature, and goes to increase it. Never will Man be honored till every chain is broken! What must he think of his race who sees its members made brutes?

Ought not men to feel deeply for great evils — Would anything but thunder wake up men?

A condition under which a human being is kept from progress is infinitely wrong. The slave cannot be so viewed as to impose respect — the humanity cannot come out to the master. He may be a pet or an animal, but not a man.

I cannot have a *right* to make a being the instrument of my enjoyment who has a *right* to seek his own.

The desire of progress is the vital principle of

human nature.   Slavery is death to *hope*.   It has no future.   That human beings can be gay under such a lot shows the death of the soul.

· Suppose men were too debased for freedom. They are bound to be free, — bound to rise from their debasement.

No man has a right to sell himself forever. — There can be no equivalent.   Certain rights are inalienable.

The advantage of freedom is that we may be ourselves, not bear the stamp of another ; and this is implied, that the individual will be a higher and happier being than if formed by any one.

War.

What is a declaration of war but a devotion of two countries to every evil which power and passion can inflict !

In war our gain is our brother's loss, — our success his misery.   When we triumph, he mourns. A benevolent mind must weep amidst success.

That human beings should deliberately destroy one another and call this glory !

Shall man desolate God's works? Disciples of the prince of peace, — shall we destroy one another!

Self-Culture.

Greatness is inward sovereignty. He who is not shaped by innumerable influences, — but bends them all to the ends of the moral nature, — he is great.

Self-reverence is not reverence of what we are, but of that higher nature, which reproves and condemns and abases us.

There is in us that which is greater than we can be, — which is not personal but universal.

Do we not rise to a love of ourselves, such as is utterly unknown to a selfish man, — such as we experience towards an excellent friend? We become our own *friends*. He that is dazzled by outward things probably has not learned *himself*.

A spirit of self-sacrifice, — a willingness to lay down life itself, — not a spirit of self-torture, — but the *power* of *love* overcoming ease, pleasure.

We have to expect suffering when we oppose the world. Let this not discourage.

I am to give myself, not to be carried by *storm*, — not to be driven or drawn by others in a manner implying the diminution of my own activity.

Self-government and self-sacrifice are one.

He does not understand self-sacrifice who does not desire to conceal it.

Is there no danger of our self-control degenerating into tyranny? A man may lay severe rules on himself as truly as another may.

It is *exclusive*, not excessive, love of self which makes the difficulty.

Have we no reason to fear when we make a man happy by processes promoting our own interests?

It is kindly appointed that in becoming selfish we become miserable.

We desire love that we may be sustained in our own good opinion, — for self-flattery. How much injury we receive from those who love us without a moral basis!

In wishing people to devote themselves to our enjoyment, we call them to a low work. — We should wish them to propose a higher object, — a divine good, — that which is universal.

To diminish the influence of pain and pleasure over the will, to be able in the presence of both to choose the right with our whole energy of soul — this is noble and to be sought.

Each man has *his* own modes of viewing and expressing things. These are worth all others.

Some through sloth, fear, or self-indulgence, put themselves into the power of others, — give up the will ; — this is base. The surrender of the will is virtuous only when virtue is the end. We ought to decide and resolve on the fullest development of our nature. To give up ourselves to others to be guided, controlled, and so forth, is to betray our trust. We are to learn from others what is well and good, when they are better instructed ; but so far as our own powers will serve us, we should use them.

The man who is ready at every moment to sacrifice all to duty and bear the cross, — he is crucified to the world, at the moment of possessing and enjoying it.

The danger is that people will not see with their own eyes, — speak with their own lips.

The passion for belonging to a mass is strong in us all.

Individual life, — energy, — that favors coöperation as nothing else can.

Independence, — not a proud, unkind scorn of men, — but a moral independence, — should be our aim : — and for this we should contract our wants, resign desirable situations, so as to avoid the need of sacrificing ourselves to another's rule. We must give no man rule.

A man should make nothing for himself only.

A mind, rapt, absorbed in God and other beings, so as to forget itself, never to recur to itself, hardly seems sane.

Nothing injures more than a feeling of inability.

There is nothing trifling : — people are trifling. I know no trifling amusements. I know many trifling people. It is not the amusements which are trifling, but they who give their minds to them, who suffer a round of amusements to fill life and the mind.

True sport is but a change of activity.

Is not the mind to be made strong by exposure? Must it be housed, nursed, kept within limits? May it not be trusted amidst all kinds of opinions? Let it associate with the wise as *friends*, but, like Jesus, dine with *sinners*.

The use of books, travels, etc., is to free us from the bondage of the near present and pressing — to break old restraints.

We are all able to know what is essential, but not to know that we do not make essential what is not.

Fellowship.

We want such views of humanity as shall shake the soul to its centre. Not a fierce, but tender, as well as burning love. Even indignation should have a tone of deep sorrow. In Jesus was there not a perpetual sweetness? He passed from indignation to greatest tenderness. His lament for Jerusalem closed his denunciations.

It is true that every soul has its own warfare to go through, but still we may help one another.

A feeling of constraint is a sign that we are

not in a congenial atmosphere. — Wherever we cannot open our souls freely we are hurt.

We must feel that we never receive so much as when we impart, for what we give comes back richer, more precious. We throw into spiritual circulation what will flow again through our own souls.

Not a being should pass through my mind without moving some love, good wishes, prayers — without some union with him. Let this be the case when rivals or enemies enter.

Censoriousness is repulsive — men are won, not so much by being blamed, as by being encompassed with love.

Dying spirits are around us. How much more affecting than dying bodies!

The question is, what can be done by all-consuming desire to do good, — by the action of intense absorbing love to our fellow-creatures? — can they stand before it?

Whoever considers himself as having any claim on God above others fatally errs.

None can enjoy God's favor but by believing that he has no favorite.

To live with the world, and know the worst of it, — and yet hope and strive for its improvement, — taking courage from God, — how much nobler than to dream of the millennium in our closets !

Take men not *from* the *world*, but from the evil in it. We are not to keep distant from the worst. God is always with evil.

When I meet a being whom I cannot serve I know my ignorance.

There is a mode of existence, thought, belonging to this earth. Should we gain by anticipating our future state? We do not want the child to be a man.

Ought the man to be an *angel ?*

How great the crime that prevents the body from becoming the powerful minister and expression of the mind, — that dims the brightness of the eye so that it ceases to pierce men's souls, — that takes away the vigor of thought by indulgence!

Mutual dependence supposes strength in each part on which the other may lean.

When men become, as they call it, independent

in condition, they become more dependent upon opinion.

We all lean on one arm.

Influence.

No man is to be a copy of another — even of the best.

Outward things act upon us not so much according to their own natures as according to our own.

Must we be swayed wholly from abroad ? We are told what to say, to think, to do. Cannot a man move and grow from within ?

Every human being whom we approach should be the better for us.

Men sometimes work themselves into a fever because they see others highly wrought. The zeal of imitation is very common.

Excitements which draw men together in masses, and increase their power over each other, are of doubtful character.

You ask what are your vices to me? I answer, *much.* I am a man acted on by other men. I am influenced by all around. There is one human heart. There is no neutrality in the warfare going on between Heaven and hell — virtue and vice.

Men do not listen to a man who fears them, who is not above them, on whom *they* act.

They must feel him acting on *them.*

Human censure, scorn, acts on us precisely in proportion to the importance we attach to human judgment.

We, ourselves, give to others' contempt its chief sting.

Human nature recoils from force. It cannot be driven. You can do no good to him who counts you his enemy.

Do we not judge most justly of people when we seem not to judge at all — when we receive impressions from the whole character — when there is an influence from the joint looks, acts, and manner?

How unlovely the aspect of what is called religion and reform! How genial, attractive, is deep love! They who would spread it must cherish it, must fill the soul with it as with an ocean.

The hope of doing good to a beloved being, of acting nobly on a noble spirit, should be a great motive.

A lovely spirit does spread.

When a vital, celestial influence comes to me from a mind which lived ages ago, — what a proof of the unity and connection of the spiritual universe!

Is will ever so impressive as when *still?* A passionate will may bend.

Progress.

We need not be what we were yesterday.

Onward is the word! To rest in any improvements is to lose them. No firm tread but by going on.

On no subject am I to stop as if it were exhausted.

All human greatness is but a pledge of human progress. Admiration assures it to us if we are but faithful.

Self-imitation is not *growth,* and the beauty and fervor of sentiments wither by an exact repetition.

There may be progress from *love* of *motion,* which amounts to little. Progress, to be noble, must have a noble Idea.

The primitive right of a being is to improve his condition. To keep him where he is, is an invasion of his highest right.

The power we possess is the seed of all we are to possess. The unbounded energy of virtue hereafter is at once a fruit and recompense of our efforts here.

So to work that we shall unfold ourselves and grow to greater sacrifices, loves, hopes, and joys — this is the Perfect for us.

We must forget what is behind. If we cease to originate we are lost. We can only keep what we have, by new activity.

To see clearly, to get out of the mist!

We cannot comprehend what is to be unfolded by the culture of Love, Virtue, Piety. The *Heaven in them* passeth knowledge.

Charity — Benevolence.

We are creatures of sympathy. We catch each other's feelings.

Dependence on sympathy may be as dangerous as pecuniary dependence.

Much of our sympathy is weakness! We shrink ourselves from pain, and we place ourselves in the condition of the suffering, — and then overflow with compassion.

It is the mark of a superior mind that it can see the grounds or germs of its own superiority in all, — can see what is noblest in itself universally diffused, — can see signs, promises, which escape others' eyes.

Benevolence when habitual becomes a cordial, cheerful glow of the soul, lighting up the countenance, delighting in all expression of good.

Relief of suffering is the best office man can perform. Should not this lead us to acquaint ourselves with the miserable?

Benevolence finds an infinite object in the universe. It is conscious of deficiency. It struggles for diffusion and goes wider and wider forth.

There is no depth of guilt or misery to which charity will not descend, — no form of humanity so loathsome with which it will not ally itself. It acknowledges kindred with everything human, it is attracted by woe, — may I say, by sin.

Character — Energy.

What grandeur may lodge in a small form if it express purpose ! — The eagle in the clouds.

To us, fastened to the earth and bound to it in proportion to our weakness, — *soaring* is power.

Force of purpose — concentrating the mind on a noble work — sacrifices to this, — have we not here the elements of all greatness ?

Force belongs to a calm confidence in truth, — in its majesty and power.

Nothing is to be done without boldness and strength.

What we want is a strong, positive character.

A man should be *felt*. He always is, when he has a self-subsistent energy.

The true force of character leaves other people at ease, — has no intimidation in it. It is immovable, but does not wish to move others, except through truth and lofty motives.

Character *is* recognized after all as the great thing. When a man dies and all his accidents have fallen off, we enquire what he *was*.

The greatest boldness ought to appear in our measures, that we may redeem gentleness from the imputation of fear. The blustering have least courage.

Nothing which is done for a man constitutes his worth, — but what he *does*, — his own energy.

The capacity of awakening activity in other minds is godlike — is worth all others. Of this we need to be conscious.

Explorers of truth have been ever active. Plato, Bacon, have they done nothing?

A man is to *act for* higher activity. Everything at war with activity is to be resisted, — then sensuality especially. Also *over activity !*

Merely to bring out a thought for pleasure is a
low end, — for self-praise, still lower.

✗ The great power is in *action ;* — this converts,
quickens, is life-giving.

Friendship.

A friend is he who sets his heart upon us,
is happy in us, and delights in us, — does for us
what we want, is willing and fully engaged to do
all he can for us, on whom we can rely in all
cases.

A friend gives himself to his beloved, and the
higher his excellence, the richer the gift.

Friendship imposes no yoke on its object, has
not the feelings of a patron, expects no compli-
ance with its opinions, no sacrifices of personal
independence, — but is jealous for the rights, dignity, and moral independence of its object, and
takes pleasure in the free judgment and elevated
spirit of a friend, only expecting these to be tem-
pered with kindness.

It confers favor, but so as to show that it is the
party obliged, and never thinking of any recompense beyond the happiness of its object.

Our friends must regard us as called and bound

to look first to the law within, and to follow this in utter disregard to their wishes. We should want friends to incite us to be victims to humanity, to be more than *their* friends.

True friends have no solitary joy or sorrow.

The attempt to make one false impression on the mind of a friend respecting ourselves is of the nature of perfidy.

Sincerity should be observed most scrupulously.

It is one of the wretchednesses of the great that they have no approved friends. Kings are the most solitary beings on earth.

True friendship, founded on moral qualities, is utterly inconsistent with a partial, exclusive, unsocial attachment to a few. I do not love my friend unless I am sensible to his excellences when manifested in others, and unless I am attached to the cause of universal virtue.

Is mutual service the bond of friendship?

A beloved friend does not fill one part of the soul, but, penetrating the whole, becomes connected with all feeling.

The loss of a friend who loved us as another

self, on whom our hearts moved and lived, is the greatest of losses.

How far is love of the beautiful and lovely in others the great means of growth? Friendship how far the quickening principle?

We receive other souls into our own. Love assimilates, appropriates.

Sympathy how nourishing!

Friends should not be chosen to flatter. The quality we should prize is that rectitude which will shrink from no truth. Intimacies, which increase vanity, destroy friendship.

Friends are to incite one another to God's works.

Sincerity, truth, faithfulness, come into the very essence of friendship.

A true friend will appear such in leaving us to act according to our intimate conviction, — will cherish this nobleness of sentiment, will never wish to substitute his power for our own.

It is essential to friendship that there be no labor to pass for more than we are, no effort, no anxiety to hide! If anything be concealed the constant intercourse of friends will discover it, and one discovery will produce others. The idea that the heart has one secret fold extinguishes affection.

No discovery of defect in a character essentially good can so damp friendship as the suspicion that something is kept back.

Friendship heightens all our affections. We receive all the ardor of our friend in addition to our own. The communication of minds gives to each the fervor of each.

We desire the homage of an exclusive friendship. We would have others render us the most refined service, that of love. We would be preferred, which to some is better than *praise*.

When our friends die, in proportion as we loved them, we die with them, — we go with them. We are not wholly of the earth.

Other blessings may be taken away, but if we have acquired a good friend by goodness, we have a blessing which improves in value when others fail. It is even heightened by sufferings.

To be only an admirer is not to be a friend of a human being. Human nature wants something more, and our perceptions are diseased when we dress up a human being in the attributes of divinity. He is our friend who loves, more than admires us, and would aid us in our great work.

A true friend embraces our objects as his own. We feel another mind bent on the same end, enjoying it, ensuring it, reflecting it, and delighting in our devotion to it.

We cannot enjoy a friend here. If we are to meet it is beyond the grave.

How much of our soul a friend takes with him! We half die in him.

We grow by love. It is said, why live for others ? But others are our nutriment.

Our affections are our life. We live by these. They supply our warmth.

Love.

Man's glory consists very much in his capacity of being God's image — which is *love.*

Nothing is more awful than love. Nothing provokes less undue familiarity.

Love is not giving ourselves away. We are too great to be given away.

Love is the end of commandment.
Love is the true principle of immortality.

Love is not weak. Its true form is power.
Wisdom is its meet associate.

True love is the parent of a noble humility.

True love is prudent. — It is not wild, visionary,
for human happiness is too dear and sacred to be
made the subject of rash experiment.

Nothing is so free from passion as love, — for
it is *large*, wide, and far-looking.

It is the essence of love to be willing to suffer,
— to rejoice in our suffering for others. Hence
it is energy, courage, hardihood. It is not *tame*
and faint and weak.

A strong love, seizing an object firmly, ardently,
discovering the means to it, is not easily discour-
aged, — is conscious of a power treasured up in its
own fervor, — is keen-eyed to discern opportunities. Oh, what can it not achieve !

He who loves so far serves.

Judiciousness, prudence, expediency, — are
words for selfish caution and distrust of principle.
Love disclaims these, and so is wise.

Selfishness may make a compromise with self-ishness, but love never.

A narrow love is not the true love. We have not penetrated to the Divine in man.

Where is the fire of love which consumes all selfishness !

Love in the young mind is an aspiration after Infinite Beauty. How the imagination spreads over the object an inexpressible charm !

Is not perfect love perfect happiness ? Is not love Heaven ?

Love is the life of the soul. It is the harmony of the Universe.

Is life found in union, and that union love ?
We have passed from death to life.
Is death a separation — life an organization ?

Can we love those whom we undervalue? Esteem and love go together.

Individual affection always favors the freedom of its object. It loves him as an individual. It does not wish to break down his peculiarities, — to make him conform to itself.

If love is faith in the divine capacities, then the great work is to bring them out.

Love absorbing the whole nature would destroy itself. Its office is to expand the whole nature.

Is not the soul a germ of love?

Are we not to account that love the truest which respects our freedom, which lays no chain upon it, which encourages it, which leaves us free to act from our own minds?

Is not a spirit of adventure connected with true love? This naturally generates hope, for it is one with God. It has no selfish anxiety or dread. It cannot suffer. It desires to accomplish great good. It is not rash, but feels in its own promptings a divine impulse. It adventures and sacrifices more freely than any other principle.

To love infinitely is an infinite blessing.

Nor are we ever to feel that our love is worth little, if we love uprightly, justly, nobly. A virtuous attachment to another is to ourselves and that other a great thing.

If we desire a partial exclusive love, — we are then personal, partial, *selfish*.

Should we wish to be the objects of any love but what exalts the lover ?

True love has a character of confidence, boldness, freedom in social intercourse. Having no private aims, it is frank. Having no selfish fear of opinion, it does justice to its convictions. In escaping from self we escape from embarrassment.

Love — a deep interest in another being. — What a charm there is in it, inexpressible, indefinable. It is the light of life.

Love lies deeper than emotion. Emotion is but an accident.

We are happy not in proportion to what we possess, but to the affection which surrounds us. Love from a beloved being is a kind of Heaven.

What an impulse is love, — how spiritual, and of how mighty influence !

The loving heart looks into the mystery of nature. Life is love. To love is to live.

They who fly from love to be devout, are they not extinguishing piety !

We lavish affection on a few. Do we know what all should excite?

We ought to live as among spirits.

In loving all we do not love a mass, but a multitude of individuals.

Love is the parent of thought.

Will he love much who sees in our nature little capacity of excellence and happiness? Will not love sink as man is degraded?

In hating vice we must love virtue. Hatred must be a form of Love.

Love is the remedy for anger.

True love delights in all who possess it, and counts their success its own.

Courage enters into love, for love looks beyond those private interests which awaken fear.

To expose and sacrifice ourselves for private aims brings no consolation. How much comes from the sacrifices of love!

Love seeks to render objects worthy of esteem. It is a thought for the spirit's life. — Here the mystery.

The being who by an attachment lives in our minds imprints himself there more or less.

Love is the all-conquering power, and to conquer evil by good is its chief end and constant work on earth.

We show our love to our friends in vindicating their high character.

A soul full of love and charity, moved by human misery, will think less and less of private comfort.

Love alone gives dignity to self-sacrifice.

We desire to be loved without inquiring into our right to love. — We desire it selfishly. Is there not an instinctive desire of affection as food?

True love is an *active* love, not passive, not excited in us irresistibly by another, not making us submissive. We must consent to it, approve it, throw our souls into it. The impulse must be from *within*.

Gratitude does not say, " I have received so much good, I must repay it." The idea of commeasured obligation does not enter it. It would pay *more*. It can set no limit to itself. It does not think of requiting the gift, but the spirit. It sees in kindness a summons to kindness. It owes the *heart*.

Virtue.

Virtue is chainless. Nothing can bind it. Its essence is to withstand all.

We cannot be virtuous by yesterday's virtue any more than live by yesterday's life.

A faithful man wishes *all* right to be done by *all* men. His own virtue is not dearer than others'.

It is virtue which makes us at peace with ourselves, and this is essential to happiness. We do succeed in flying from ourselves. We can, in a sense, lose ourselves in crowds, in business, in pleasures. But after all we must sometimes come home. We must sometimes be left to ourselves.

Ah, what a shadow is praise ! How imperishable is virtue ! Shall I then live to draw praise or awaken virtue ?

Virtue is looking above ourselves, but selfishness uses it as a means of self-concentration.

Virtue is the soul's *own*.
It is not another's.
It is the only true property of the mind.

We admire the man of genius who describes a virtue, — how much more he who manifests it! The sculptor gives the saint, — how much more admirable the saint!

A good being attracts good will to him. He really knows how to use happiness, prosperity, the means and power of usefulness. He may be trusted with blessings.

Virtue is fearless. It belongs to the untrodden. It cannot see far into futurity. — It trusts. — It carries its presage in itself.

Who has learned perfection his end has lifted his soul to celestial virtue.

Pride.

Pride is the greatest meanness. The man has never seen, comprehended the *great*.

A supreme pride lays polluting hands on everything to build itself up.

When we become great in our own eyes, others become small.

Our nearness to ourselves deceives; the near becomes great. We are to comprehend the greatness of the distant.

We can more readily believe that we are wrong than hear our neighbor tell us so.

Almost every man finds something on which to build a feeling of self importance — complacency. — He looks around for something illustrious with which to connect himself.

Pride as well as love aspires after great, signal sacrifices.

Humility.

The just estimate of ourselves at the moment of triumph is the most eminent renunciation of pride.

The humility which comes from studying our own defects is in danger of abjectness. True humility is forgetfulness of self, in the sense of the great, the Divine. The soul is humbled by its loftiness.

Not an idea of duty but teaches humility, — not a view of nature — for it surpasses comprehension. What so strange as pride!

Humility is clear vision. It is removal of the great film which prevents sight.

Humiliation implies power, for all sin is a neglect or abuse of power. It is suffering divine power to be quenched in us. Power *measures sin*, and all pretence is abject and false any further than founded in consciousness of a great power.

The greater a man is, the less he is disposed to show his greatness. True nobility of soul rises above and suppresses the love of show.

As we value sincerity we should keep ourselves out of sight, — doing good without pride or egotism.

Flattery.

We are bound to approach men by noblest faculties. — No flattery, no soothing, wheedling, etc.

There is a softness which dishonors people, as if they could not bear plain dealing.

Do not minister to self-consciousness. True friendship never flatters, denies itself, fears to corrupt.

Love pours itself, but never flatters. It needs no verbal utterances, — a look is enough. Be not another's looking-glass.

We should look on people who give and receive flattery as giving and receiving poison, — destroying one another.

Sudden esteem ought not to be desired. Should we not be willing to wait to be known?

Vanity, — a pleasing consciousness of what is in one's self, — desirous to impart itself to others.

Fear.

No *timidity*. The mind is to rise above this. The least fear palsies.

Let the mind be fixed on too high objects to be disturbed by inconveniences.

Fear makes a man a slave to others. This is the tyrant's chain. Anxiety is a form of cowardice embittering life.

The mind subdued by terror is not fitted for self-direction.

He who carries one fear of man with him carries a weight on his soul. He cannot rise to the height of his subject.

Duty.

People should see that we expect much from them. We should in nothing let down the law of duty. — But this should be done not rigidly, sternly, unfeelingly. It should be an expression of our *respect* for their *nature*, and should tend to awaken *self* respect.

The choice of easy duties — how perilous!

To live in violation of a duty we might know is akin to the guilt of living in opposition to a known duty.

What may be right for me to-day may be wrong for me to-morrow. Some new impression, knowledge, power, may entirely vary my duty. No other is the judge.

What have we to do with the goods or evils of life when an infinitely great interest is at stake!

We cannot judge what we can accomplish till the world is given up. Every passion subtracts from our power.

Ambition, how it weakens us! Fear of man, how it palsies!

Evil — Sin.

We are sometimes angry with ourselves for sin, — *passionately* so. Remorse is often the work of irritated self-love. How different from humility!

Impulse is called nature, but an impulse unbridled wastes nature.

One bad passion taints the soul.

Vice has a ludicrous as well as an odious aspect. Benevolent satire is sometimes the best means of correcting it.

Is this the solemn view of sin, — that in violating one right we violate all right, — that in exalting the personal over the Right in one instance we do it in all, and become a discord in the Universe?

To escape present suffering, we incur future ruin.

We stay the tottering building to make a great crash.

If anything degrades a man it is passion, rage. He who being insulted loses self-possession insults himself more.

All vice is limitation. It is absorption of the soul in the narrow.

Who suffers most from sin? The sinner himself; — one would think then that sin would be most hated *for his sake.*

Every vice has its mode of treatment. — The healing art for the soul has yet to be learned.

Sensuality is the grave of the soul.

A tyrant on a throne is not so degrading as a private tyrant, whom our luxuries, or wants, or interest have made our master.

The science of mind removes Satan.

Avarice is foresight wasted, — a noble power abused, the very power which ought to secure Heaven.

Conscience.

I am to live listening to the voice in my own soul, and to no other but as sanctioned by this.

He who adopts conscience, the opening *law*, as his guide, breaks all other laws both of thought and action.   Prejudice is renounced.   Unbounded truth is his aim.

We cannot chain our future selves. — This is well.   We might obstruct growth, fix permanently our present weaknesses or narrow views.   But in following present conscience as conscience, we are doing much towards determining our minds to future following of it.   The true loftiness is a feeling that there is a divinity within us, — a law superior to outward authority, — a self directing, according to the voice of God within.

My conscience is a rule to myself only. — My will has no province but my own mind.   I am responsible for no others.   I may desire others' virtue, but must not interfere with their freedom. Each is to act from his own inward law, — each to be turned on his own soul.

I owe to myself what I owe to no other.   The care which I take of my own mind would be usurpation if extended to another.

A languor of the moral nature is most to be feared.

Conscience is an incommunicable gift.   I am a law to myself only. — It were better for a man to do a wrong act in obeying his own conscience, than a right one in obeying mine.

We have no right to be at ease, if conscience is not a friend.

It is more important to me to preserve an unblemished conscience than to compass any object, be it ever so great.

Can there be a great thought without self-sacrifice and childlike subjection to the *divine law within?*

Are we ever to say inertly — we fail in our duties? Should not this be a stinging thought?

The dying of conscience is the departing of God from us.

I have a right to judge — then a right to be protected in judging.

Faith.

Faith is love taking the form of aspiration.

Can we trust for happiness any further than we trust that we shall use well our nature?

Faith rests on every promise of God, however imparted, — directly, or by the soul.   Is not the soul a promise?

Is there a necessity of ultimate reliance on our own minds?   Faith in any truth is faith in the faculties which apprehend it.

It is said we should have no faith in ourselves. But faith in future good is a faith in our capacities, — that *we can* enjoy infinitely.

He who has kindled in my heart an affectionate earnestness has in so doing given a pledge of what he will accomplish. — Never despair under God!

To the benevolent and cheerful spirit all Nature breathes and speaks of love, of universal care, — whilst the selfish, irritable, and gloomy mind, accustomed to brood over partial evils, looks on it as a vast prison or storehouse of calamities.

There should be faith in the possibility of impressing others with our own highest views.

Faith and works.   Does this answer to spirit and letter?

Who are we that we should measure out for

ourselves? We know not what is best. We deserve nothing. This alone is best, that we leave all to Him who knows what is best.

A great man is willing to live and die with a *great* cause in the confidence that it will essentially prevail. Such a mind *hopes* generously.

The idea of manly fortitude sustains men in suffering. How much more the idea of the godlike!

A deep faith lies beneath sorrow. It does not lighten our outward burden, but gives strength, — better still.

Wisdom — Knowledge.

Knowledge is essential to freedom.

The wise become so more by sympathy than study.

All knowledge is a going forth, — an impartial judgment is a step.

To use a thing well we must understand it.

Knowledge is dearly bought if we sacrifice to it moral qualities; if, in pursuit of it, the heart is chilled.

Wisdom is not afraid to see evil in all its strength, for it looks far enough to discern the omnipotence of the antagonist power.

There are impressions, feelings, convictions, which cannot be defended by particular arguments, but which are the results of a whole life, which represent the whole past experience, in which the whole nature is represented, — the reason, heart, conscience, imagination. Is not this Wisdom?

The mind darts beyond terms, rules, — and its flashes are often worth more than labored deductions.

Truth.

Truth is correlative to being; — knowledge, to reality.

Infinite truth is before us. Why do we see only what we saw before!

Every new and noble truth, the moment it is regarded as an instrument of praise, becomes weakened, loses its hold on the soul; for the frame of mind is low, not congenial with it.

Truth from a devout voice should be heard,

though truth only chooses or makes a sweet and gentle one.

The habit of applying epithets loosely, of applying to the whole what belongs to a part, is very ruinous to our moral sense as well as to the intellect.

Unfaithfulness in one relation is unfaithfulness in more.

Every feeling or state of mind which I wish to produce in others, I should express myself. When I wish to produce conviction of a truth, I should use the tone of firm conviction. When I wish to excite gratitude, — when I dwell on the loveliness of religion, let me speak as if I *felt* it.

Truth drives those who are disposed to forsake it farther and farther. Error must be multiplied to preserve its consistency. The light must be shut out, for it discovers error.

Government may forfeit its rights, but cannot absolve us from truth.

Bad measures are submitted to when evaded by fraud.

A man might pass for insane who should see things as they are.

Inspiration.

A profound mind sees in a hint a clue to infinite discoveries. Every thought is as a seed, springing up at once into a rich harvest.

When we see justice, truth, we but allow a passage to the beams of immense intelligence.

Who has attained the true life and peace of the soul? — He into whose mind beams of the moral glory have shined.

There are deeper intuitions than we can bring out distinctly to the consciousness. Childhood is under the sway of these.

When we sympathize with a great mind — are we not inspired?

Thought — Reason.

All men have power of thinking, — not all, power of *thought*.

A thinker is at work all the time.

We know but one unity, *mind*. This is one, however various the actions.

The greatest mind escapes the present, and uses past and future to lift itself above all time.

Because we reason ill, are we incapable of reasoning? We detect the false reasoning by reason.

We are not to conquer with intellect, any more than with arms. Conquest is not kindly, not friendly.

The intellect is enthralled, darkened, by the influence, the authority, the prejudice of fellow beings. From these it needs to be saved.

Doubt requires grounds as truly as belief. We must have reasons for doubting. Unreasonable doubt has no validity. Doubt must have the authority of reason. How then can we doubt its authority?

The outward system is one of fixed laws. The mind subjected to it is confined, enslaved.

It is not a *single* thought or a thought subsisting by itself, which exerts such great power. Great thoughts are quickening, diffusive, gather others round them.

I look on the modes of mechanism, more to admire the mind than the product.

We can calculate mechanical force — not so the mind. What steam and water can move we know — but not what mind can move.

The veracity of reason can neither be proved nor disproved, for we must use reason for the process. To doubt whether reason be credible, is it not equally unreasonable? — for doubt is an act of reason.

The very question why we trust our faculties is an appeal to them.

Not a step can we take without them.

Thus skepticism, if it require a reason, is self-destructive.

Passion gives the *unbounded* to finite objects. Reason sees and bounds, and makes the finite yield to the infinite, — the temporary to the everlasting.

We determine our modes of thinking in determining our course of life.

Every one knows that there are tones which, without reference to what is said, give an immediate impression that the speaker is deficient in intelligence — so there are tones of thought.

Conversation.

Studied conversation is most tedious and defeats all its ends.

We want in conversation that the heart should flow out.

We cannot every moment pronounce a maxim.

Converse so that you may draw largely upon other minds.

Speak with the animation and elevation of one who hears the great theme.

To establish a quick communication between the heart and countenance and voice is what we need.

Too often the voice is mere air, charged with no soul, — a mechanical effect.

He who governs his tongue is perfectly able to control all his passions.

Never talk for show. This rule will almost cut up conversation by the root, — but no matter.

The mightiest leaders are those who stir up other souls to the same deep original activity. Eloquence often injures by forcing, not leading, the hearer to reproduce.

On common topics we should present the best thoughts which immediately occur to us, in the best language which immediately offers. Simplicity, sincerity, and truth will often be the only commendable qualities. We shall say nothing new or striking.

On every topic we may express love to God and man.

Our thanks are due to an orator, because he raises us above our ordinary perceptions and feelings — gives us to see with a new eye, to burn with a new fire.

He who converses without the idea of displaying himself has made great progress in humility.

It should always be one end to benefit those we converse with. If we cannot give much, give little.

Unless conversation be pleasing and active, people grow weary and love each other less for meeting.

Conversation should flow from the heart, and the tone of the voice as well as the countenance should express affection.

A Christian acquainted with God should talk as becomes the acquaintance. A man shows his society everywhere.

It is very important that in conversation we have a pervading sense of the dignity of the being with whom we converse.

Conversation should not be rash; but, intending uprightly, and feeling generously, we should speak boldly. Selfish timidity should not cramp the expression of our sentiments. We had better err sometimes than be perpetually cramped. A generous stream may overflow and injure, — this is better than stagnation.

Will not new modes of activity offer themselves to him who has new aims? Will not a new soul breathe through his life?

How does soul flow into soul by speech, eye, etc.! What a noble gift, the communication of soul!

Just in proportion as men advance in civilization they give more time to conversation.

Let your life fortify your conversation.

People converse with carelessness. They wish

to say something, and this leads them to say anything.

By aiming to become too useful we may become useless. Conversation is designed to benefit us, like air and water, insensibly.

When we consider that the essence of human society is communication of thought, it will be hard to find a vice more hostile to society than falsehood, or the perversion and confusion of those signs by which men agree to communicate their thoughts.

The art of being silent at proper times is worth acquiring.

Conversation confirms the temper it expresses.

Making fine sounds is the ruin of eloquence !

Our conversation should do good by its general spirit, not by its anxious confinement to the most edifying subject.

Does not the pleasure of talking over old things arise from the rapid associations, the trackless glances of thought, — the flow of ideas experienced in such a conversation ?

The chief use of preaching is to convey *living impressions.* We want truths quickened in men's minds where they be dead.

Take away all but that conversation in which the parties do not aim to make impressions favorable to themselves, or to exert talents which will strike themselves and others, and how silent the world will be!

Woman.

How many ways to the heart has woman!

Until we know woman, we know not *strength* of *love.* In this we have perhaps the best emblem of omnipotence as well as divine goodness.

Woman is the dwelling place of religion, and communicates it to the young.

Women soften our character and yet make us heroic. The same traits of character produce these different effects.

It is said woman loves courage in man that he may protect her. No — she loves courage which makes sacrifices. She loves heroism. She loves protection, but from a hero's arm. It is the virtue, not her own safety, she loves.

Man forsakes Christianity in his labors, — woman cherishes it in her solitudes and trials. Man lives by repelling, woman by enduring, — and here Christianity meets her.

How wisely is it constituted that tender and gentle women shall be our earliest guides, — instilling their own spirit!

A family bound together in love must be most pleasing to God, — it must be the nursery of all good affections.

Woman made for man, — beautiful, touching truth, — suited to an age of female degradation!

Children — Education.

The birth of a child is one of the most important events in the universe. All other things are created to perish. The oak grows from the acorn to live many years, but it will decay. The monuments may survive centuries, but will moulder. Even the sun will fade. But the soul will live and will make everlasting progress.

We ought to look on children with almost awe, — to feel their greatness.

Every child has a right to means of spiritual life.

You would shudder at the thought of mutilating your children, of wounding them, feeding them with poisonous herbs, exposing them to contagion, but there is something worse than all these. No wounds are like those of the soul.

Set your child before you. Say, this child is born for eternity — he is capable of knowing God.

It depends on *you* whether your connection with your children is a blessing or a curse.

Fear makes children false.

May not punishment supersede conscience?

Children are learning when in good society.

Teach your children as they advance that you are fallible; — encourage them to think for themselves.

Have reason to think that what you teach is true.

How much dead matter is put into us — idle, lifeless knowledge which the soul never quickens, which comes and goes unchanged! No vital union takes place between it and the mind. — Is this forming or loading the mind?

Consider not what the child does, but the motive, and strive to rectify this. Be not satisfied with producing obedience by mere power. Ask — is the obedience from principle and feeling, which will cause its durableness and prepare him for self government? Strive as much as possible that he may govern himself.

Is not the child the best judge of what its faculties require? — at least we should select from objects which it evidently takes pleasure in.

Injudicious restraint is the parent of self-will.

Great wisdom of God is seen in limiting parental influence. The hope of the world is that parents cannot make their children all they wish.

The child is born for love and with a thirst for it.

How many children are injured by scolding, ill temper! There is a beauty and contagion in sweetness of temper.

When I play with a child, render it kind services, sensibly increase its pleasure, I confer a present good, and I do more ; — I help to form an affectionate spirit.

Do not judge of a child's pleasures by your own

feelings. A disappointment trifling to ourselves may be an infinite evil to the little being whose whole soul is wrapped up in the pleasure removed. A child's little plan should be respected.

How cautious should a parent be that his children never have reason to suspect or distrust him!

Pursue what is practicable. Do not try to make your child a wonder.

To form children to kindness, let them see it.

Education is as important to the child as culture to earth. You are too wise to expect crops without planting; — it is just as rational to expect improvement without education.

Home, — the nursery of the Infinite.

Youth has more positive enjoyment and less happiness than any period of life. It is restless, uneasy, expecting everything and disappointed continually.

Manner.

Manner should be a sign of ideas.

Perfect self-possession, — arising not from high

opinion of ourselves, but from moral superiority to opinions, — this is the true manner. This is carrying reverence for virtue into common movements.

No error in manner is so bad as having *too much manner*, or as mannerism, — an appearance of having studied manner, of thinking about it, of being full of ourselves. Complete absorption in our subject is the perfection of manner!

A free, bold manner, the expression of our strong convictions, an earnest activity, coming out naturally and with generous confidence in truth, — how graceful and noble are these!

The soul should speak in countenance and motions. This it is which impresses. We have aimed in vain to substitute excellence of composition for manner.

Some people are polite in manner, but they let you see that they know it. They think more of themselves than of you in paying you respect.

Mildness of manner is indispensable, but our sentiments should be expressed just as they are.

Repose is the perfect balance of all the powers.

There is never so much novelty as when the new is seen in the old.

Habit.

The customary passes for the necessary.

Habit not merely confirms but freezes what we have gained.   It gives a dead stability.

If in doing an act we saw a chain winding round our bodies we should be alarmed.   But habit binds chains by every deed.

Subtle habits of thought are the most dangerous.   How the *I* pervades all things!

Habit is the common principle of consistency. Is there not a nobler one, — the principle of simple reverence to truth and duty without being anxious to be consistent?

He who breathes free air enjoys more than in perfumed chambers, — so he who drinks water, — and the poor man may see God.

Art — Genius — Ideals.

Art is a spiritual triumph.

The poet who sees and feels life's development has higher knowledge than the philosopher.

We say — the generations pass, but the works survive. No, — the genius of Michael Angelo is more immortal than St. Peter's.

That is a work of genius which partakes of the eternal and unchanging, which is not local or temporary but becomes the principle, the key, the illumination, the soul of the mutable and passing events, which arrests us, which associates itself with all we see, and is confirmed by the development of time and our own nature. — Shakespeare is as a prophet whose writings are fulfilled by all which takes place.

The poet has the perfect in view even in delineating the evil. — The highest, purest form of a quality, the *most distinct* embodying of it, is his end.

In Drama it is the greatness of the soul in its agony which interests us, — a mighty feeling, a depth of woes laid open.

Statues, pictures, — breathing a celestial Love and Power, — are not these of use to reveal to men the divine glory which is to be sought and loved?

Genius is seen not so much in paradox, as in its living, renovating, freshening conception of a plain truth.

The book gives the *ideal*. But to get the ideal from actual life is the great thing.

The great advantage of art is that it saves labor. This we need. Human life is too much spent in toil.

Men of active business and social qualities escape from reveries. Perhaps the possession of the mind by external things is no great advantage. Practical men, — never led astray by imagination, — are they the most valuable?

Is it not possible to be an impersonation of the highest principles, — to realize our high conceptions, — to live in the world of Ideas, and to show that they are *practicable?*

For how little do most of us live! How low the ambition, — to interest and please a society! Is life to pass away without leaving any effect?

We must have an end beyond the present work, — this is rising above an occupation, in a just sense.

Let not fame be thought of. Only propose a lofty end and be prodigal of self, of reputation, in pursuing it.

The abundance of poetry now may show rather the greatness of demand than the delicacy of the prevalent taste. We consume too much to be nice.

Life.

We must not waste life in devising means. It is better to plan less and do more.

Life is a journey, and he who has least of a load to carry travels fastest and most happily.

Life should be held loosely, — in readiness to be yielded up with a martyr's spirit.

Life is a fragment, a moment between two eternities, influenced by all that has preceded, and to influence all that follows. The only way to illumine it is by extent of view.

Life is a bringing out of the infinite depths of the soul. — That which now keeps us down shall lift us up.

The evil of life consists not so much in doing bad things as in being without ends, — acting from impulse and acting from *others'* minds.

The mysterious life is not that which is afflict-
ed — etc. — but the prosperous, monotonous, self-
indulgent, in which nothing generous is awakened.

May we feel that no life is short, which has
fulfilled the end of life.

When we give ourselves to mutable things, we
become parts of the material system, — slaves,
subject to outward laws.

To *live*, — to have spiritual force, is the grand
thing!

May the false colors fade from life, — and at
the same time may we not forget the value of
life, but be grateful for it, and see in it a school
for an endless being.

Is not the whole of life to be a sacrifice? Even
its pleasures, relaxations, may fit us to toil, suffer,
and die for man.

Death.

Shall we weep for those who have done weeping!

We give death its terrors. The soul does not
die. What was it we loved in our friend? On

this depends whether death shall be an evil or good.

We rejoice in the belief that there is no impassable gulf between us and those who have gone before.

We rejoice that the grave has become a place of rest — death a passage to immortality.

May we think of death not to sadden life, — but to learn the true glory of life.

Suffer us not to love this life as our only existence, as if nothing were beyond it.
May death spiritualize our views.

Death teaches that our friends belong to a higher being. — Our appropriating spirit is rebuked.

We suffer through the finite. — Is it that we may look to the Infinite ?

Peace.

Peace is the fairest form of happiness.

Our office is to be peacemakers, which we are to fulfil by breathing love.

There is indeed a peace on earth, — but it is not the peace of inaction, of prosperity. It is the peace of him who accepts the conditions on which life is given, — who girds himself for the conflict, — who has a clear, strong faith that conflict is wisely ordered, and who has an earnest, in the energy it calls forth, of the perfection of his soul and the triumph of a higher *world*.

There is no peace but in subduing the enemies within the soul. Hostile principles involve War. We must subject the soul to sweet concord.

Some persons are contented and easy from the extreme simplicity of their desires. — They are satisfied with little and with what is easily attained because other good excites no desire.

This is only insensibility : — it approaches the peace of a vegetable, — not of God who is infinite desire.

Joy — Happiness.

Enjoyment is good to him who looks above it.

This thirst for happiness, — is it not a promise of full streams ?

Has a man a right to throw away his own happiness any more than that of another ?

Pleasure may perfect us as truly as prayer.

Moderation in pleasure, or absence of all *dependence* on it, is essential.

Everything depends upon the *habitual exercise* of the mind on a higher order of good. We cannot rise from a life steeped in pleasure, to the conception of that good which annihilates pleasure.

There is a joy which adorns life, — the overflowing of delight in beauty, in intellectual power, in those we love.

There is no religion in being unhappy.

Happiness is not a gift, but an object to be secured. Are we not then to study it? Happiness is not to be advanced by anxiety about it. A spirit of confidence seems necessary to it. We are to watch over it by a kind of *neglect*.

Some, having found the Supreme Good and, in it, an inexhaustible fountain, living waters, are relieved from all anxieties, are superior to evils, and have all their capacities of pleasure quickened. — He who has no fear but of doing unworthily is in the true way to light heartedness.

We begin by expecting happiness from something outward. This is the delusion of childhood and of the infancy of human races. The progress of the mind consists in nothing so much as in the development of the consciousness that happiness has its seat and foundation *within.* Till we learn this we are ignorant indeed.

Joy comes from having *great interests*, not from idleness, — from great affections, not from selfishness, — from self-sacrifice, for this knits souls, — from great hopes.

Joy belongs to health of souls, and to health of body.

Some minds are light by the absence of all great thoughts and interests. They think only of trifles. Nothing weighs upon them.

Others are light through their own elasticity, energy, — and never lighter than when pressure calls for elasticity. This is the true light heartedness.

Ought we always to be meditating on our own and others' sins, — to be solemn? Is there not something strained and suspicious in that virtue which renounces the ordinary pleasures of life?

Enjoyment through moral energy, through voluntary exclusion of depressing thoughts, through grateful opening of the mind to good, through desire to shed joy around us, is noble, and such is meant to be the joy of life.

Happiness, meaning a deep, full, affectionate joy, is a most lovely thing.

Oh! the joy of enjoying, with the reflection that God and all good beings approve and partake our joy!

Sorrow — Pain.

Sorrow has its dignity. The individual forgets himself in his interest in another. — It is a sign of the extension of our being.

Every life has some severe pain. In such events the soul aches through and through. The arrow pierces it. Its whole nature is suffering.

Mere suffering will not do us good. — Mere tears will not wash a living sin. The very severity of suffering leaves us harder, — a solemn thought. We may grow insensible.

The mass of men are content with escaping pain, — and with animal good. How they acquiesce in death!

Pain, whether in this or the next world, is a low, selfish motive. Will not the character built on this motive partake throughout of its poverty?

We cannot, if we would, benefit others by per-

petual pain, hardship.   We cannot endure it : —
our nature forbids !   God is not willing.

Pain is nothing if not wrongfully inflicted, —
if it does not shock our moral sense.

Destiny.

Our steps tend somewhere.

We move along the earth-path and do not feel
it ; so every moment we change our position in
life, yet seem to remain in the same circumstances.

In vain would human weakness throw off the
iron necessity which is laid on it.   Suffer we
must.   Fight we must, — or sink and perish.

A man thirsts for opportunities of knowledge
— which are withheld.   Nature denies him an
eye to see with. — Poverty dooms him to toil.

Matter — Spirit.

We are bound by chains of matter.   Are we
not to burst these ?

We are to escape the limits of space and time.
What is most noble is not related to them.
Truth is eternal and universal.

A spiritual body raised in power is one which the soul informs. A glorified body is one through which the soul radiates, — which it uses, — which in no measure governs it.

Will the wicked be placed under the power of matter, — a hard tyranny, self chosen? Is it through moral conquest that we are to rise above the laws of matter? May the soul take the spiritual body out of these just as life now suspends chemical laws?

We are related to the Universe by thought, which needs this boundless whole, and delights in discovering Unity ; — by love, sympathy, reverence, by will, energy, *power*, which are awakened by the consciousness of vast connection and design.

All nature has sprung from spirit, — is an expression of it, — has spiritual connections. Is the natural then to be opposed to the supernatural?

The Soul.

A great thing to have a soul in health!

The body is to die, and then the spirit is free. Are we not in this sense to die daily, — to liberate the spirit from the body?

All weakness is unspiritual; — all emotions which master us are such. Delicacy is not debility : it shrinks from the gross, not from the strong.

May we not come to feel sickness, darkness, coldness of the soul, as truly as of the body ; to know when we are in the light, when the sun shines upon us, and when we are in darkness ?

The spiritual in common life, — this is the great discovery.

Wealth may come to us by inheritance or chance, — not so inward life. We may sustain the body with little thought, — but not so the spiritual life.

We idolize wealth, for we know not how great the soul is. We have nothing with which to compare it.

Looking into our souls — seeing what is health, what harmony, what the disorder of sin — is a great means of awakening *power*.

Cannot the soul endure as much for duty as for honor, or through pride ?

Christ commanded. Does not the soul too command *all* men to be just and holy ?

Is the soul as much wounded by sin among the ignorant as among the enlightened?

The soul can and must do nothing which degrades or stains it.

Be just to the soul. Study it. Grow more conscious of its higher action.

To look into the particular soul is the great sagacity.

A great thought strikes through the soul,—dissolves old connections, establishes new, revolutionizes the mind.

We are spirits too. To feel this is to act in harmony with spiritual worship.

Always in proposing a truth, aim at its reaching men's souls and working mightily.

There is one great office in life,—that of Soul Quickener.

Passiveness is the death of the soul. Is any evil so great as this!

The being we are nearest, we know the least of. We are ignorant of what is within.

To form a fine statue from the stone is nothing compared with bringing out beauty, proportion, from the soul.

Some flowers open at sunset and close at sunrise.
So some souls bloom unseen.

The multitude, sunk in matter, cannot judge the spiritual man. He is not to expect any justice from them. They know nothing of whence or for what he lives.

A godly jealousy over our own spirits, regarded as of divine origin, belongs to us, and we must not so give them away to others as to narrow or cast them down.

I believe we have a power over the soul by which we can take it in a great degree out of the power of external things.

We belong not to this world only, — to all worlds. We have connection with all spirits. When the soul is pierced by the loss of *one* friend, does not our vast connection comfort us ?

Aspiration — Prayer.

Looking up is our strength.

To look far forward we must gain an eminence.

And now that Thou art doing so much for our happiness, may *we* not betray it.

We must not expect to be understood if we soar above the world.

Suffer us not after so many sicknesses, changes, and death of friends, to live heedlessly.

Seek always in the Universe *Unity, harmony,* — and, in these, *God.*

Give us simplicity, godly sincerity ; teach us to avoid false pretences and to be true to our convictions.

Whilst friends live may they show us, in all that is good, Thy goodness : when they die, may they carry us to Thee.

From the loss of our friends teach us how to enjoy and improve those who remain.

Let it be our happiness this day to add to the happiness of those around, to comfort some sorrow, to relieve some want, to add some strength to our neighbor's virtue.

Let the employment of this day leave no sorrow, no remembrance of wrong, at night, but may it be holy and profitable, blessed and innocent.

High aims, ends! Nothing low, selfish, — nothing tame, mechanical, — no bending to low standards. — Bringing the mind into contact with high, generous, pure, holy spirits, — not to yield to them, but to be kindled by them.

A great Idea lifts us above the power of evil. We can suffer for it. It is something impersonal.

A habit of prayer becomes mere formality unless we begin with the heart.

Are we to pray that God will make us holy by his immediate agency, any more than that he will make us rich?

God — Religion.

Nothing is supernatural but the divine. God is above nature. He is *the supernatural.*

God loved the world, — and how did he exercise that love; — in sending his son to fill it with *love.*

God is the happiest being in the universe. Can we not become happy by sympathy?

Not he who talks most learnedly of God feels most his presence and perfection.

God thinks of all beings. — So should we.

We would see more of God because what we now see is so glorious !

He who studies nature and denies God is as a man who reads a book and denies that it had an author.

I believe in God : — with this conviction I go abroad and meet him everywhere.

Man would confine Thee to his church, — would subject Thee to his interests. We adore Thee as Infinite.

Many traverse Heaven without meeting God there !

The soul is a chaos, without form and void — dark. God, — truth, — is the light, is the brooding spirit. The elements obey new affinities and arrange themselves into harmony, beauty.

It is the glory of God that he answers to the love of Infinity in the soul.

God speaks to us through the holy souls in which he dwells. Our sympathy with them is sympathy with God.

God is an ever developing Thought, the living water in us.

I am a child of God. I hear him described in language which shocks me. I hear acts ascribed to him which would disgrace a human sovereign, — acts unequalled in the record of tyranny. Shall I feel nothing ?

I am sure Christianity will endure because it is founded on man's nature, — answers to his deepest wants, — his essential and noblest wants.
I do not say that what we now call Christianity is to live forever. I think not — I hope not. Christianity is obscured, — almost lost.

What a bond a great truth is ! This was the glory of Christianity. It substituted a spiritual for an outward bond.

Men have labored for churches more than for religion.

The church is meant to make the free spirit, to aid its flight to God, not to subject it to *man*.
We have no forms in domestic life. Friend-

ship has none. Is not religion more free? The heart has its own mode of utterance, free, spontaneous. The soul is too great for forms: to bring it out is the end of churches: — machinery keeps it in.

Where now is the strength of the Catholic Church?

The name of Fénelon is a shield for his whole church. The virtue of that single soul is more than hosts.

We live in sight of religion as men do of the heavens or of stupendous mountains. An admirer of these, — a man who lives to them, may awaken our sensibility to them.

It is as incongruous to profess religion as to profess benevolence.

The adoration of goodness, — this is religion.

Sin is not a distinct subsistence. It is the mind affected in a particular way.

The *right* to which we are bound is not *insulated*, but connected and one with the infinite rectitude, and with all the virtue of all being. In following it we promote the health of the universe.

What! are the great fundamental truths of religion so obscure that intelligent men miss them!

What are called saints are not the most estimable.

The world is so full of wonder that the wonderfulness of a future life is no argument against it.

Our religion is laid in a corner. We think it much if a man, on any occasion, acknowledge it. Instead of appearing like the life it only discloses itself occasionally.

Is not the spirit bound down by the world in which we live? How we speak and act with reference to what is around us! So did not Christ. He gave out a nobler mind.

The anchorite, rejecting the outward for a dream of mysticism, erred. It must be rejected for true greatness, sanctity, — for distinct perfection.

True piety does not play the hero, — does not walk with solemn strides, — does not feel itself too great or good for any of the irreproachable pleasures of life. True greatness is akin to happiness and unlocks the springs of joy.

The right, beautiful, happy, true. — Are not all these one, — or different aspects of one reality ?

Holiness is the soul powerful over the senses, — free, unslaved by sense, clear to see the Divine, powerful to forsake all for it.

In serving each, we serve all, and ourselves as bound up with the living whole.

We see a special Providence in *means* coming unexpectedly, — in unexplained coincidences. If there be a miracle, why are means used ? If we may pray for one miracle, why not for another ? If for a miraculous cure, why not for patriarchal longevity ? What bounds can be set ?

To ask for what we want is no virtue. We shrink from asking men, and the less we ask, the better. — Prayer regarded as a mere expression of desire has no *worth*.

A universe requiring endless pain for its security ! Is not this blasphemy against its author and against holy spirits ?

Infinite, endless punishment would make hell the most interesting spot in the universe. All the sympathies of Heaven would be turned towards it.

Sensation.

Sensation is the first stage of the mind's development, the first affection of the soul, the beginning of our inward life.

The spirit is unfolded by its connection with the body. It is deeply indebted to the material organism with which it is allied.

Sound as we hear it from the great masters of music, as it comes to us charged with the thoughts and feelings of noble souls, does not seem to us unfit for Heaven; and the beautiful lights which are spread over creation, who of us does not hope to enjoy them forever?

It is not a nerve which sees or hears. It is *I* who see and hear. Sight and hearing are capacities of my soul.

We place the smell of the rose in the flower as its permanent abode. We place heat in the fire and sound in the harp, and suppose them to issue from these seats, and penetrate us through our organs. But in all this we cheat ourselves. The heat, the fragrance, the sound are in ourselves, are simply affections of the mind. The Aeolian harp simply vibrates, — the melancholy sound, which seems to swell from the instrument, belongs only to our own breast.

Sensation belongs to the mind as truly as the most abstract thoughts and refined affections.

We are apt to speak of sensations as flowing in upon us from the outward world. The truth is that they flow from us and furnish the Universe in its ever-varying robes.

We create what we delight in, — the soul transmutes the colorless, silent, cheerless earth into a paradise.

Nature, by impulses on the organs of sense, invites the mind to pour forth her boundless treasures, — and obedient to the summons the mighty enchantress sheds over heaven and earth, spring and autumn, cloud and ocean, a profusion of beauty which she cannot herself comprehend.

The sensualist and the spiritualist may both lay down their arms and cease their useless warfare. If they come to understand one another, they will find that they differ in little or nothing.

No matter how an idea or mental affection springs up. — I can conceive of myself as so constituted that on the first impulse of light on the retina an intuition of God would have sprung up in my mind. With the first vibration of air on the ear, the idea of duty might have dawned on me. These grand convictions would have lost nothing of their grandeur in consequence of these

occasions of their appearance in my mind. —
Ideas and feelings are to be estimated not by
their mode of birth, but by their nature, and their
correspondence to reality.

The soul is an unbounded force, seeking perpetual expansion, and if left to itself, it would
break out into a chaos of sensation, thought, affection and will. It needs restraints to determine
the order of its development, and to give it the
possibility of moral self-control. The body, I
apprehend, is ordained by God as this restraining,
regulating power.

By union with the body the soul's activity is
not created, but confined. The body is a prison,
as the instinctive wisdom of all ages has taught,
curbing the soul's action, except in particular
directions and under particular conditions.

Instead of regarding sight and hearing as pro-
ductions of the optic and auditory nerves, it may
be proper to say that we are now confined to see
and hear by these organs only.

It is astonishing how little we owe to the senses
of what we trace to them. The world, as first
revealed by them, is almost wholly different from
the world we daily see.

That the soul is capable of other sensations be-
sides those we experience, I cannot doubt ; that

only five classes of sensations exist in the universe is most unlikely. The spirit is probably susceptible of an infinity of sensations as well as of thoughts.

Pleasure and pain are the earliest links of thought. Through these the soul first discovers infinity. In childhood it grasps a good beyond what it finds. A secret restlessness and discontent disturb the morning of life.

The indications of a vast good mix with our earliest pursuits.

Pleasure and pain are also the first occasion of the action of the moral nature. — Through them the great struggle between desire and duty commences. Our moral history dates from their collision with our sense of right.

In this view what an important place they hold in the spirit's development! — Sensation, — the first occasion of moral energy and moral triumph !

There is no greater sign that the whole of life is our infancy than the fact that physical pain and pleasure keep us so much in motion, and are designed to place us under higher excitements, to sever the will from desire, to unite it with rational and moral impulses.

This is the soul's manhood, — but as yet how slowly have men made this progress !

Musical sounds call forth emotions within us which we experience from no other cause.

They seem to wind their way into depths of our nature which nothing else can visit. — Not only sounds, but certain combinations of color have a sentiment, if I may so say, and speak to the soul. There is something spiritual, too, in certain odors, — in the fragrance of the fields and flowers.

Even the lowest of all our sensations, that of taste, will, I believe, in a better age, when the animal nature is subjected, rise into a degree of dignity.

The blue sky, the green fields, the hue and fragrance of flowers, the splendor of the rising and setting sun, and of the stars — how deeply do they work in the wise and pure soul!

What springs of thought and emotion do they unfold, — and how much of the happiness of the happiest may be traced to these influences!

The eye and the ear may become to us almost perpetual inlets of purifying pleasure, and the senses which at first chained us to this world may unlock with magical art infinite prospects beyond the world.

The I or Self.

Every man knows what he means when he says "I" "myself" — he knows nothing else so well. Words cannot help him. The " I " cannot be analyzed. There is nothing more simple into which it can be resolved.

Consciousness is like *life*, — that which we all feel, which is infinite reality, — and which eludes our grasp and seems to vanish into a word, when we strive to define it.

Life is revealed as something permanent. Our thoughts and sensations indeed are changing, and often fleet through the mind with the speed of lightning. But the " I " is the same. The joys, sorrows, hopes, fears, purposes, efforts of the past day or year may have gone never to return, may have perished forever, but I, who joyed and sorrowed, exist to-day, am one and the same as yesterday.

It is this permanence of the I, which gives unity to our shifting lives, which binds into one our vast and varied experience, on which responsibility is founded, which puts us in possession of the past and the future, and is the condition of endless progress.

Perception.

The ends which the mind proposes determine the direction of its perceiving power. The philosopher, having for his end that great spiritual

Idea, Truth, subjects the material world to the keenest inspection, and detects in its phenomena the signs of unseen laws, and makes it a new world to his *age* by the truths which he associates with it.

So the artist, with the idea of Beauty to inspire and guide him, analyzes and groups anew the prospect which is a blank or confused, unmeaning expanse to a common spectator, and lives in the midst of an order and glory which his own spirit creates.

How much do we owe to this power of external perception! We are introduced to a magnificent inheritance. The universe becomes our property. The sublime heavens are our own. A kind of omnipresence is bestowed on us. We transport ourselves to other worlds.

From scattered observations we construct the solar system, and get glimpses of the order of universal nature.

How grand, how awful, is this creation of God!

But there is something grander, and that is the spirit which can comprehend it, which can construct, unfold within itself, the Idea, the Image, of this boundless whole.

It must not be supposed that it is the grandeur of the Universe which makes the soul great. — This would be lost on us, were there not an inward grandeur corresponding to the outward.

A noble school is profitable only to noble spirits. The learner must have something great in order to receive great lessons.

The universe is to us what we make it.

It is the soul which aggrandizes nature.

Reflection.

Most men for the want of turning the mind on itself live in great ignorance of its common operations.

They understand the motions of objects around much more than the movements of their own souls.

The inward world is a dark, confused, ever tossing ocean, and, through the obscurity and confusion under which the mind appears to itself, it is able not only to live in self-ignorance, but to practise imposition on itself, — hide its true motives from its own eye, — to ascribe to itself such as do not exist.

What we call discoveries are generally expansions of confused images or thoughts which have long pre-existed in the mind.

Every man has within him treasures of wisdom which he does not suspect, — precious ore imbedded in crude thoughts. His power of inward perception, like the infant's eye, glances over the surface. What is passing within himself he does not know. The volcano of passion is perceived at moments of eruption, but its deep workings are unseen.

We look down into the abysses of the soul with feelings of awe, resembling what are experienced on the brink of a precipice, whence the descending gaze sees at vast distances no bottom but a silent ocean of cloud.

This power of introspection is of inexpressible dignity. By this we become acquainted with spiritual existence, — we enter the spiritual world.

This glorious universe, of which material nature is the dim expression and semblance, is first revealed to us in our spirit. We enter it through the portal of our own soul. Even God is manifested within us. — The infinite Mind has impressed his image on ours, and through this alone we know him.

Intelligence, wisdom, power, love, joy, beauty, — these are intelligible to us through the dawning within ourselves.

By looking within, we find in the confused mass of our thoughts the elements of the grand thoughts of God.

It is wonderful that such a power as this does not impress us by its grandeur.

One would think that the temptation to plunge into this invisible world, and forget what surrounds us, would act on some minds at least with irresistible power. But such is not our destiny, and this spiritual asceticism would defeat itself. The mind by living within and watching itself perpetually would arrest its own flight and free expansion. Men, for want of reflection, too often waste life, and turn it not only to unprofitableness, but to bitterness.

Conception.

The life which turns all to nourishment is the soul's, and through this alone outward things do us good.

There is an immense difference in the power of conception in different individuals. Some men's minds are picture galleries, filled with images of what they have seen, heard, etc. — The past springs up to them in the vivid colors of reality.

They are painting all their lives.

Relation.

Our knowledge of God, man, the universe, may be reduced very much to relations.

If God existed in utter, necessary disconnection

from all other beings, where would be his omnipotence, omniscience, infinite love and impartial justice ?

Strip man of his relations, and what do we leave of him ? He has no private, no public history — no purpose — no progress — no good.

The mind can divide itself among many objects and its range of simultaneous thought continually increases, and in this we have a pledge of the vast domain to which thought is to extend itself in the progress of our existence.

The world stripped of its relations or manifested to us only in disconnected fragments would be stripped of all its glory. All beauty consists in proportion, harmony, — that is, it is in relation, so that the charm is derived from within. The world is a manifestation of God, is a sphere of human action, is a source of wisdom, only so far as its relations are discovered, — that is, so far as the mind invests it with its own treasures.

Memory.

Time is first revealed to us as *the past*. The faculty which recognizes this begins its action in the earliest stages of our being. We wake up and find ourselves plunged in this mysterious stream, always flowing, never beginning, never ending, and bearing us onward to unknown worlds.

The idea of time to which memory introduces us is one sign of the greatness of the mind.

It stretches out into the infinite. It awakens our interest in all which has been, and all which is to be.

By a few hints which geology furnishes, we go back thousands of centuries, while hope and fear rush into an endless future.

Nothing which has entered into our experience is ever lost.

The mind has infinite stores beneath its present consciousness.

The past is acting on us by a silent influence.

There is a far deeper life and motion within us than we can distinctly comprehend. The past is living in us when we think it dead.

In the future life, the mighty volume is to be opened, and we shall derive ever-growing wisdom from the dim, faded experience of the passing day.

DATE DUE